THE SCOTTISH JOKE BOOK

Lang**Syne**

PUBLISHING

WRITING *to* REMEMBER

Lang**Syne**

PUBLISHING

WRITING *to* REMEMBER

79 Main Street, Newtongrange,
Midlothian EH22 4NA
Tel: 0131 344 0414   Fax: 0845 075 6085
E-mail: info@lang-syne.co.uk
www.langsyneshop.co.uk

First published 1987. Reprinted 2006 and 2010.
This edition published in 2013.
Printed by Fixture Displays, China.
© Lang Syne Publishers Ltd 2013.

ISBN 978-1-85217-105-6

THE SCOTTISH JOKE BOOK

Jokes compiled by Wally McKinley,
with cartoons by
P.D. MacDonald and Dave MacMerry.

LangSyne
PUBLISHING
WRITING *to* REMEMBER

Dedicated to my granddaughter, Roxanne

Facts of Life

Two wee boys on the bus.
One says "Are you three or five?"
Other one says: "I dunno."
First boy says: "Do you know anything about sex?"
Wee lad says: "No."
"Well you're three" says first boy.

★ ★ ★ ★

Plastic Bliss

My wife had her credit card stolen.
I haven't reported it, though.
The thief's spending less than she did!

★ ★ ★ ★

"IT SEEMS TO WORK — HE'S NEVER HAD AN ACCIDENT"

Job spot

A man threw himself into the River Clyde.
A man spotted him and dived in to the rescue.
The first man shouted "Leave me alone, I'm committing suicide."
The second man paid no attention and continued to swim towards him.
"I told you, I don't want to be saved" shouted the man.
"I'm no' going to save you, I just want to find out where you work."

★ ★ ★ ★

EVERY TIME I HEAR THAT BOY LAUGH I REMEMBER THE DAY
THEY TOOK AWAY HIS FATHER!"

"I WOULDN'T WANT TO DRIVE SOME POOR MAN OUT OF HIS MIND!"

★ ★ ★

"YOU'VE BEEN DRINKING — YOU ARE REEKING OF BREATH-PURIFIER!"

☆ ☆ ☆

Pure genius?

Irishman on Mastermind.

Question: Name?
Irishman: Pass.
Question: What's your specialised subject?
Irishman: Fish.
Question: You've got twenty seconds to name a fish beginning with 'S'.
Irishman: Single!

Boom! Boom!

A pal of mine got a finger transplant and his nose rejected it!

"WHY NOT BASH HIM ABOUT THE HEAD WITH YOUR
HANDBAG — THAT'S WHAT I DO!"

Heid-case!

I used to work with the council, sweeping the streets.
On the first day I went up to the foreman and said "The
heid's come off ma brush "
'Right", he said. "Here's another one."
I went up to him the next day and said, "The heid's
come aff the brush."
He said, "Here's another one. And if it happens again,
you're fired.".
I went up to him the next day and he said, "Has the
heid come aff the brush?"
"Naw," I said. "The handle's come aff the brush "

Boom! Boom!

A woman complained to her doctor that she had a lot of wind, so he gave her a kite.

"IT'S THE SORT OF THING THE VICTORIANS MIGHT PUT IN A CHRISTMAS CRACKER — PROBABLY IMPORTED IN BULK FROM CHINA".

"YOU CAN'T BE ON THREE DIETS AT THE SAME TIME!"

Inside Story

Once upon a time there was the skunk family. Mummy skunk, Daddy skunk and two baby skunks. In and Out were their names.

Whenever In was out, Out was in and whenever In was in, Out was out.

One day Mummy skunk said: "Where's In?" "In's out", said Out. "Well go and bring In in", she said. So out went Out to bring In in.

Eventually Out appeared with In.

"How did you find In?" asked Mummy skunk. "Easy", said Out. "In-stinked!"

Second Class

The old lady was skint.

So she thought she would write to God and ask him for some money.

So she wrote: 'Dear God, please send me £100 as I am skint.'

She sent the letter through the Post Office.

The Postmaster got it and thought "That's a shame, so it is.'

So he organised a collection among the staff.

They raised £95, which they sent on to her.

The next day they got a letter which said: 'Dear God, thanks very much for the money.

'You were £5 short.

'That'll be those swines at the Post Office.'

"OH GOOD, CHARLES! YOU REMEMBERED TO GO TO THE BANK!"

> **Knock, knock.**
>
> There was a knock at the door. My wife answered it — there were two policemen standing there.
> "Does Wally McKinley live here?" asked one of them,. 'Aye", she said, "Bring him in.'"

"DOES THIS MEAN YOU NO LONGER CARE, ANDREW?"

Wife's Tale

I met ma pal coming out of the butcher's. He said, "Ah just got a pound of mince for the wife." "By God", I said, "You got a bargain there."

Bad sign

Man went to the doctor and said "Give me something to make me sweat." So the doctor signed him off.

"HAS THE BEST MAN GOT THE NOOSE, I MEAN THE RING?"

★ ★ ★

"LET'S FACE IT! IT'S NOT GOING TO FLY ANYWHERE!
YOU'VE BEEN CONNED AGAIN!"

Money! Money!

The Rabbi in the Synagogue asks his congregation how much they earn.

A man stands up and chants: "I am a joiner and I earn £100 a week."

The congregation stand up and chant: "He is a joiner and he earns £100 a week."

Next an electrician stands up and chants: "I am en electrician and I earn £120 a week."

The congregation stand up and chant: "He is an electrician and he earns £120 a week."

Then this fellow in a gold lamé suit stands up and says: "I am in a pop group and I earn £2000 a week."

The congregation stand up and sing: "There's no business like show business."

☆   ☆   ☆

"THIS IS THE SAFEST PLACE TO HIDE — THEY'D NEVER THINK I'D WANT TO COME HOME TO YOU".

"THE OLD DUKE WAS MARRIED FOUR TIMES!"

★ ★ ★

"NO SMOKING, PLEASE!"

Boom! Boom!

Man on TV quiz show.
Question: "What was Rudyard Kipling famous for?"
Man: "Well, he made exceedingly good cakes."

"YOU'LL DO YOURSELF AN INJURY IF YOU KEEP PULLING IN THE GUT EVERY TIME WE PASS A YOUNG LADY!"

Boom! Boom!

I went to the doctor and said, "Ah'm no well. Ah've got a dull pain."
So he gave me a bottle of Windowlene.

"IT'S ALRIGHT, THANKS! THE DISREPUTABLE CHARACTER
CASING THE JOINT IS MY HUSBAND WORKING IN THE GARDEN".

★ ★ ★

"DUDLEY, WILL YOU COME AND LEND A HAND WITH THIS
STUPID DOG OF YOURS?"

"WHAT A SWINDLE THAT WAS!"

Sun spot!

Man went into an optician.
He said, "Ah canny see very far wi' these glasses."
The optician took him outside and, pointing to the sky,
said, "What's that up there?"
The man said, "That's the sun."
Optician said, "How far do you want to see?"

Wired in

I've got a new car.
It runs on electricity.
Very cheap to run.
I drove from Edinburgh to Inverness for 60p.
Mind you, it cost me seventy thousand pounds for
the flex.

"I HOPE YOU WILL BE EQUALLY CHARMING WHEN
YOU TRY TO COLLECT THE INSTALMENTS!"

"IT DOESN'T MENTION YOUR NAME. IT JUST SAYS THE ACCIDENT
WAS CAUSED BY A STUPID PEDESTRIAN!"

Lie-test!

Why can ghosts never tell a lie?
Because you can see right through them!

. . . .

Small Wonders!

Who are the world's tiniest ladies?
Molly Cule and Milly Metre!

. . . .

Cover Story!

Joe fell into an upholstery machine.
Now he's fully recovered.

. . . .

Song numbers!

What has eight feet and sings?
A quartet!

. . . .

Spirits galore!

My brother puts hundreds of people in touch with the
spirit world every week.
He's a barman!

. . . .

Chips are down!

What boils up, peels, chips, takes a real roasting but
never cracks?
A spud.

. . . .

Gone fishing!

I found a tadpole in my soup and complained to the waiter.
He apologised but explained that the fly was taking a well-deserved holiday.

....

Trunk route!

Why did the elephant cross the road?
Because the chicken decided not to go out that day.

★ ★ ★

☆ ☆ ☆

"ALRIGHT! THREE FALLS AND THE LOSER GOES

FOR THE FISH SUPPERS!"

Well oiled!

Police are following a car.

The driver is giving all signals, keeping well into the side of the road, driving at 29 miles per hour, giving way to pedestrians.

The panda car pulls alongside the car and a policeman says, "Look sir, you're the best driver we've seen in this city for many a year. Congratulations."

"Aye", said the driver, "You've got to be careful when you've had a few."

☆   ☆   ☆

"STAND THERE AND LET ME DRINK YOU IN — JUST IN CASE
I SHOULD EVER THINK OF COMING BACK TO YOU!"

Food for thought!

I went to a reception because I was told there would be a running buffet. Right enough — they served prunes and All Bran.

"SHE'S TERRIBLY HOUSE-PROUD!"

★ ★ ★

"STRAIGHTEN UP AND PAY ATTENTION!"

Canned!

Lady went to the doctor and told him she had burned her feet. "How did you do that?" asked the doctor. "With a tin of soup" she told him. "How do you mean?" asked the doctor. "I took it home and it said on the label, 'stand in boiling water for 10 minutes'!"

A fishy tale!

A fishing boat at sea searching for Moby Dick sees a small dinghy nearby.

The skipper shouts across, "Hello wee man in the dinghy. Have you seen Moby Dick?"

"What's that you say?" replies the wee man.

"I say, have you seen Moby Dick, wee man?"

"No", replies the wee man, "but I've seen The Sound of Music."

★ ★ ★ ★

"I REALISE NOW IT WAS THE GLAMOUR OF THE TRAFFIC WARDEN'S UNIFORM THAT GOT ME!"

Going cheep!

My wife wanted a white budgie for her Christmas.
I tried all over Edinburgh.
Eventually I found one in a wee shop in the Grassmarket.
It was in a cage beside 500 other budgies.
I said to the shopkeeper: "Look, if you get that budgie for me, I'll pay you what I paid for my turkey, how's that?"
"You're on, mind you it'll be very difficult."
So he went into the cage.
About 20 minutes later he came out, covered in scratches and blood.
"Look", he said, "Here's your white budgie. Now, what did you pay for your turkey?"
I said: "Fifty pence a pound .... weigh it!"

Jag joke!

What do you call a man who goes to the circus and watches all the clowns?
A Partick Thistle supporter.

☆   ☆   ☆

"I WAS DRIVING! — MY HUSBAND ISN'T VERY GOOD AT IT!"

"Madam, I suggest you admit your age and concentrate on denying the other charges".

"But I don't want to be a juror — can't I be a witness instead?"

"Frankly, diminished responsibility is your last chance".

"Madam — giving your husband 'twenty years in the poky' is not my idea of a divorce settlement".

Poverty is ....

*W*e slept eight in a bed. I never knew what it was to sleep alone till I got married.

Poverty is ...

*W*e never got taken to the Waxworks. Ma mother just used to let us look in faither's ears.

★ ★ ★

"MADAM, YOU ARE A GEM! MOST FOLKS WOULD HAVE LEFT ME IN THE GUTTER!"

"WHAT IS AN OLD BAT LIKE YOU DOING IN A PLACE LIKE THIS?

Christmas crackers!

I hung up me socks at Christmas, and the tree died!

*   *   *   *   *

Wee Henry was always swearing. His mother told him that Santa Claus wouldn't come to him.
"I don't believe in Santa Claus anyway. It's like the devil — it's your father all the time" he told his mother.

Henry kept on swearing. His mother decided to teach him a lesson.
So she went to the local farm and got a large bucket of horse manure.
On Christmas Eve she filled his sock with the manure.
Henry gets up next morning and looks at the sock.
He goes into his sister's bedroom and asks: "What did you get?"
She says: "I got a doll, and a doll's house. What did you get?"
He said: "I got a horse, but it ran away."

Commons sense!

There will be no nativity play at the House of Commons this year.
They couldn't find three Wise Men

*　*　*　*　*　*

A golfer hung up a pair of socks on Christmas Eve.
Next morning he found a hole in one.

*　*　*　*　*　*

Boom! Boom!

Confuscious say:
"It's a wise Eskimo who never eats yellow snow."

Boom! Boom!

What a bust up!

"Have you seen Dolly Parton's new shoes?"
"No."
"Neither has she!"

"YOU'D THINK THEY'D BE ONLY TOO PLEASED TO HAVE THEIR FURNITURE RE-ARRANGED PROPERLY!"

HEARD ABOUT THE IRISH ...

Farmer who chased a chicken on to the football pitch after the referee blew his whistle for a fowl.

Letter writer who wrote on fly-paper. He wanted it to go by air mail.

Shellfish which kept bumping into other fish and pebbles. It was accident-prawn.

Optimist who ordered lunch in a restaurant even though he'd no money. He asked for oysters and hoped to pay with a pearl.

Scholar who played truant from a correspondence school. He sent them an empty envelope.

Saver who thought he could increase his bank balance by looking at it through a magnifying glass.

Flu victim who was told to stay clear of draughts for a fortnight by his doctor. He asked if it would be OK to play Snakes and Ladders!

Legal expert who was asked to define the word illegal.
He replied: It's a sick bird.

Dog owner who lost his pet in the forest. He put his ear to an oak tree and listened to the bark in the hope of tracking down the animal.

Dunce who thought a well-read man was a healthy Red Indian.

News programme on television called ''Looking Back.'' It starts at 8 o'clock and finshes at half-past seven.

"I ONLY WISH ALL MY CLIENTS WERE SO EASY PLEASED!"

☆　　☆　　☆

"MY! SOMETHING SMELLS GOOD! IT MUST BE COMING
FROM NEXT DOOR!"

"TEN O'CLOCK AND ALL IS FAR FROM WELL!"

Wife's tales!

My wife said to me: "I'd like to look over some fur coats. So I took her to the zoo.

* * * * * *

My wife said: "Look, I'm tired of that old car. Can we no' get a foreign vehicle?"
So I got her a rickshaw.

Chinese cracker!

Two Chinese brothers came over to Scotland to work.
They got a job right away — Mr Ho and Mr Lee.
Mr Lee worked in the mine taking miners down the pit in the lift.
Mr Ho got a job in the supplies office.
One day Mr Lee went missing.
They couldn't find him anywhere.
He couldn't find his China!
The Fire Brigade were called to search for him.
Suddenly he jumped from behind a rock and shouted, "Supplies, supplies!"

"YOU'LL HAVE TO ZIP UP YOUR ANORAK AND GET OUT AND PUSH ME THROUGH!"

★ ★ ★

"HE'LL HAVE TO WAIT UNTIL WE FIND A SUITABLE PLACE!"

Fast gags ....

My next door neighbour's Irish. He was out with his two dogs the other day. I said "Are these Jack Russells?" "Na", he said, "They're mine!"

* * * * * *

I was an unwanted child.
Do you know, even at my christening they used boiling water.

* * * * * *

I was the only wean in my street that had a pram with no brakes.

* * * * *

Ma wife's got a criminal record y'know.
Oh aye — it's Sydney Devine's latest.

* * * * * * *

I watched Sydney last week.
There he was singing "'The Road To Dundee."
There was a woman sitting in the audience crying her eyes out.
I said, "Missis, are you from Dundee?"
She said, "No son. I'm a singer."

* * * * * *

I was at a right tough school. We got one holiday a year — Al Capone's birthday.

"You waste all your time and energy in mindless acts of destruction and vandalism — ever thought of being a surveyor?"

"My client was imprisoned for his beliefs — one of them being that he wouldn't be caught".

"SMILE, EVERYBODY — SAY FEES"

"LOOK MOM! THERE'S DADDY!"

Nutty!

I met an American in Sauchiehall Street.
He said: "Excuse me, Scotty, you see that building over there?
Well back home we have a building ten times that size."
I said: "Right enough, you'll need it pal. That's our looney
bin."

Minty Me!

I was rushed to hospital
They took an X ray and thought I had a hole in my heart.
Here, it was just a Polo mint in my pyjamas pocket.

Potty!

When I was in hospital the nurse came up to me and said "Oh
hello. Are you wanting a wee bed pan?"
"Aw", I said. "Don't tell me I've to do my own cooking as
well."

Oh no ... !

I'm on a Valium diet now. It doesn't help me lose weight but most of the food falls off the fork before it reaches my mouth.

* * * * *

Two drunks in a fish and chip shop.
One turns to his pal and says "Has a lemon got legs?"
His pal said, "Naw."
"Aw hell", the first drunk said. "Ah've squeezed the budgie on to ma fish."

* * * * *

Two Irishmen are on a plane.
Seamus turns to his pal and says: "If this thing turns over will we fall out?'
"Naw," says his pal. "I'll still talk to you."

* * * * *

Irishman walks into the chemist and says "What's that wee white powder on the counter?"
Chemist says, "Askit."
Irishman says, "Wee white powder, what are you?"

I went into the grocer. I said, "Give me fifty pence worth of Swiss cheese." He wrapped up three holes!

* * * * *

I was singing in a club last week and a woman tried to commit suicide when I was singing. The bullet just missed me by a couple of inches.

* * * * *

Man goes to his doctor.
"Can I have more sleeping tablets for the wife?"
Doctor says, "I gave you three dozen last week."
Man says, "I ken, but she's woken up."

* * * * *

Police stopped a driver and asked him to blow into the breathalyser.
He blew into the bag and two horns came out the side of it.
"What have you been drinking?" asked the policeman.
"Bovril" said the driver.

"MUM, WHEN PUFFS OF STEAM COME OUT OF THE SPOUT DOES THAT MEAN THE WATER IS READY?"

Boom! Boom!

I'm a member of a Jewish golf club. It's been open for twenty years and nobody's lost a ball yet.

Boom! Boom!

I love my mother in law. I'd love to smother her in diamonds — but there must be a cheaper way!

Oh dear ... !

Things are very bad the now — even contortionists can't make ends meet!

* * * * *

I walked into the butcher — I said "Have you got a sheep's heid?"
"Naw", he said, "It's just the way Ah part ma hair."

* * * * *

I learned the Wedding March backwards — now I only sing at divorces!

My neighbours think I'm a good singer. They broke all my windows last week just so as they could hear me better!

* * * * *

I only learned two songs y'know. One is God Save the Queen .... and the other one isn't.

* * * * *

I don't drink at the moment — I think I've got gout. At least every pub I go into the manager shouts "G'out!" at me.

Ice cool!

I met my wife at the pictures. She was selling ice cream. See the day we got married. She walked down the aisle backwards.

Eye! Eye!

Man with glasses goes into pub. Says to barman, "I'll bet you a pound I can bite my right eye."
Barman says, "Right, you're on."
The man takes his eye out and bites it.
Barman says, "I bet you a tenner you can't bite your left one."
Man says, "Right, you're on."
So he took out his teeth and bit it.

In the soup!

Wee Hughie got a job in a restaurant.
Customer comes in and asks, "What kind of soup have you got?"
Wee Hughie made a noise like a chicken. "Good," said the customer, "I'll have a plate of that."
So Hughie brought him a plate of mushroom soup.
Customer said, "That's no' chicken soup."
Hughie said, "Ah canny do an impression of a mushroom."

Drinks galore!

Wee Tam goes into a Glasgow pub with his head inclined to one side. "Give everybody in the bar a drink and a pint of lager from me."
The barman poured the drinks and said, "That'll be £41.25."
Tam said, "Ah've nae money".
The barman said, "If you'd done that in the bar next door they would have broken your neck."
Tam said, "I've just come outa there."

"I'M AFRAID YOU'LL HAVE TO GO TO THE GREENGROCER FOR THE SPRIG OF PARSLEY!"

Boom! Boom!

I've given up drinking. I promised my eyes a white Christmas.

Boom! Boom!

I remember the time Moses came to Edinburgh. He did the sermon on the Mound!

★

Taxing!

I got stopped in Princes Street by the police. I said, "What's wrong?" "Your rear light's not working". said the bobbies. So I gave it a kick and it went on. "There you are, it's working OK" I said.

"Now try kicking your windscreen" he told me, "and see if it'll bring your road tax up to date."

Good try!

I remember the Pope came to visit Edinburgh.
He arrived at Murrayfield rugby ground.
Thousands of people were there including Ian Paisley. A policeman said to him, "What are you here for?" Paisley said, "I've come to convert the Pope." "Ah well," said the cop, "You can go away home. We've taken the goalposts down."

"YOU HAVE WON MY HEART, RICARDO! CATCH ME!"

★ ★ ★

What a drag!

When my car broke down the garage charged me twenty five pounds to tow it three miles home.
I got my own back though. I kept the brakes on all the way.

Whisky sour!

When I get a cold I just buy a bottle of whisky and in two hours it's gone ....
The cold? No ... the whisky.

'SEEING YOU ONCE A MONTH IS GOING TO MAKE THE
NEXT TWO YEARS A LOT EASIER".

Stainless steel!

Doctor: "You'll really have to go on a diet. Tell me, what's your job?"
Patient: "I'm a sword swallower.'
Doctor: "Well, you'll have to stick to knives and forks for a while."

Blind Logic!

Drunk in bar to equally sozzled pal: "Jimmy, listen to reason. Why don't you take a taxi home?"
Jimmy: "No use — ma wife wouldnae let me keep it in the house."

Heard in class ....

Teacher: Tell me, Jason, where is Timbuctoo?
Jason: Er .... betwen Timbucone and Timbucthree please, miss?

....

Teacher: Caroline, tell me the one word in the entire English language that is pronounced wrong by everyone.
Caroline: Wrong.
Teacher: Correct!

....

How do you get snappy answers? Cross a maths teacher with a crab!

......

Teacher: Mark, where is Melbourne?
Mark: In Australia, sir.
Teacher: Excellent. Now, tell me .... where is Sydney?
Mark: He's not too good sir, ... at home in bed, with the mumps!

....

Teacher: In this test I want to see who has the best imagination by telling me a real whopper of a lie!
Jimmy: I swam the Atlantic twice, the Pacific four times, and climbed Everest backwards.
Billy: I saw him do it!

....

Teacher: Horace, what is a Norseman?
Horace: Easy .... a fellow who rides an 'orse.

**"SEND THEM A BILL FOR A MILLION — THEY'LL THINK
WE HAVE A COMPUTER".**

Roll out the barrel!

*A Scotsman and an Englishman went up Mount Everest. It's
very dangerous, Everest — they've got double glaziers, you
know.*

*The snow was coming down heavy. The Scotsman said: "This
is the finish — we'll never survive this."*

*Just then a big St Bernard dog appeared with the barrel round
its neck.*

*The Englishman said: "Ah, here comes man's best friend."
And the Scotsman said: "Aye, and look at the big dog that's
carrying it!"*

"PROBATION? NO CHANCE. IT WAS HIS LORDSHIP'S CLERK'S HOUSE YOU DID OVER.

★ ★ ★

Only fools ....

The place is so small they don't have a village idiot .... they all take it in turns.

And Dracula ....

Did you hear about the man who opened Dracula's coffin? He got a bat in the mouth.

"NO CHRISTMAS WHEN I WERE LAD — FATHER WORE BLACK
TIE & CLAIMED SANTA HAD DIED IN'T NIGHT".

Lost and Found!

Two golfers on the course.
One says to his pal: "What do you think of my special golf
ball? You never lose it. If it goes into a burn it floats to the top
and bleeps. If you play in dark conditions it lights up, you
never lose it. If it goes into the rough it rises to the top and
bleeps."
His pal said: "That must cost a bomb, eh?"
"I dunno. I found it" replied his pal.

"... DRIVING WITHOUT LICENCE, INSURANCE, M.O.T. & HAVING
CONSUMED 4,548,842,003 SHERRIES ..."

War dance!

General Custer at the Battle of Little Big Horn. Custer is lying on the ground with 45 arrows in him.
He turns to his captain and says: "I'll never understand Red Indians. Just twenty minutes ago they were singing and dancing."

Close shave!

I walked into this hairdressers in Glasgow.
"Will you give me a shave?"
"Aye", he said,
So he started shaving me.
Well, he cut me in about six different places.
After he finished I said, "Could I have a glass of water please?"
"Are you no' feeling well?" he asked.
"No, I just want to see if I leak" I said.

Roaring drunk!

I was at Edinburgh Zoo with my kids recently.
There were two drunks looking at the lion's cage.
The lion came up to the front of the cage and let out an almighty roar.
The first drunk said, 'Hey Jimmy, are you comin' hame noo?"
His mate says, "Naw, Ah'm gonny wait for the big picture."

Meet the wife ...

My wife went to a fancy dress ball as Lady Godiva.
The horse got more dances than she did.

*   *   *   *   *   *

Then she entered a beauty contest. She came second .... a pig won it.

*   *   *   *   *   *

My wife bought a mud pack. For two days she looked marvellous .... then the mud fell off.

*   *   *   *   *   *

I met our milkman. He was telling me that he's been out with every woman in our street except one. I told the wife about it. She said: "Aye, it must be that stuck up bitch next door."

I gave my wife a new Jaguar for Christmas .... it chewed her to bits!

"MY BROTHER'S GIVEN UP ESTATE AGENCY — HE'S GOING STRAIGHT!"

Twincredible!

I had a pal who was an identical twin.
What a life he had! Every time his twin brother did
something wrong, my pal got the blame, so he did.
At school, if the brother got his lessons wrong, my pal
got the strap.
My pal fell madly in love with a beautiful girl.
What happened on the day of the wedding?
She married his brother.
But he got his own back. Last week, my pal died .... and
they buried his brother!

"DON'T BE STUPID, HIGGINS! PUT DOWN THAT CHAIR AND LISTEN TO ME!"

Some leak!

An American took a Scotsman on a sight seeing tour of the States.

He showed him the Grand Canyon, the Empire State Building etc.

Each time, the American said: "I jis bet you don't have anything like that back home in li'l old Scatland."

By the time they got to Niagara Falls the Scotsman was fed up.

Looking at the water cascading down the American said: "Ain't that jis wunnerful?"

"Aye", said the Scot. "Mind you we've got a rare wee plumber back home who could fix that for you."

Job spot!

Sign on Job Centre Window: "Wanted, youth for position as Human Cannonball .... must be willing to travel and of the right calibre."

A fair stretch!

*Did you know that copper wire was invented in Aberdeen.
It was all through two Aberdonians fighting over a penny.*

High-flier!

*There was a lot of trouble at the circus. The man on
the flying trapeze caught his wife in the act.*

Tee up!

I used to be a caddy at St Andrews.
An American asked me to caddy for him.
He stood on the first tee and the rain bucketed down.
Anyway, he was in every bunker in the first nine holes.
At every bunker he took a wee flask out and had a swig
from it, saying: "God-dam country."
At the tenth tee he said: "Is there no dry place here at
all?"
I said: "Well, you can try the back of my throat."

**"I THINK YOU SHOULD FORGET ALL ABOUT TEACHING THIS
FELLOW A LESSON AND TRY AND MAKE FRIENDS WITH HIM!"**

"I PUT THE LOVE POTION IN HIS PORRIDGE LIKE YOU SAID, BUT HE WENT OUT AND BOUGHT A SPANIEL PUP".

★ ★ ★

What a blow!

I'll never forget my first wedding.
Somebody had left the church door open and the wind was blowing right up the aisle.
The wind blew the music off the organ.
The wee lady organist bent down to retrieve it.
She had a mini skirt on.
The minister quick as a flash said: "Any man who casts his eyes upon that unfortunate woman will be struck blind."
I says: "Here, I think I'll risk ma bad eye!"

★ ★ ★

Pie-orities!

There was a notice on the pub wall which said 'Ploughman's lunch 50p'.
I said, "What's this ploughman's lunch?"
The barman said, "It's a pint and a big pie and half an hour upstairs with the barmaid."
"Ah," I said, "Whose pies are they?"

Heard about ....

The woman with the tuneless voice who sang to her two budgies and they died from shock. It was a case of killing two birds with one tone.

....

The shipwrecked sailor who after being rescued told his wife how he'd lived on a can of sardines for a week. She thought he was very brave not to have fallen off.

....

The vanishing flea-circus. A dog came in and stole the show.

....

The man who knocked down a house with one blow of his hammer. Yes, he was the auctioneer!

....

The convict jailed because he told the truth. The judge asked him if he was guilty and he replied, "Yes m'lud."

....

The fellow who bought a horse and trap for fifty pence. It was an old clothes-horse and a mouse trap.

....

"IF YOU'VE SEEN ONE YOU'VE SEEN THEM ALL!"

☆ ☆ ☆

Oh no!

I went into a shoe shop and asked for a pair of size 9 shoes.
"Try them on for size" said the assistant.
So I did.
"They're too tight" I told him.
"Try them with the tongue out" he said.
"They're shtill too tithe" I said.

★ ★ ★

Dead men ....

They say Aberdonians are mean.
My grandfather was an Aberdonian.
See this ring.
He sold it to me on his deathbed.
I paid him by cheque!
When he died he left all his money to the unknown soldier's widow.

"STRIPEY SEEMS TO HAVE GOT MARRIED IN THE BICYCLE SHED!"

"I'VE A GOOD MIND TO CLOSE THIS PLACE DOWN!"

Ear 'ere ....

I went into this pub and there was a fellow sitting there and he had only one ear. I felt kinda sorry for him so I said, "Would you like a drink?" He said, "I've got one 'ere." So I didn't buy him one.

Impediment of reach ....

You can always tell an Aberdonian. He's got low pockets and short arms.

Too clever!

I went for an audition for Crossroads and failed. I remembered all my lines.

Paradise lost!

Man went to psychiatrist. He said, "I feel like a coconut."
Doctor said, "You're Bounty."

"REALLY, MEG! DO YOU HAVE ANY IDEA WHAT THESE PEOPLE CHARGE PER HOUR?"

"THERE'S SUPPOSED TO BE A SECRET DRAWER SOMEWHERE CONTAINING THE TITLES TO A FORTUNE!"

★ ★ ★

Tall story

Fellow is taken into hospital. He had swallowed a thermometer. It never killed him, but on a warm day he was six feet ten!

☆ ☆ ☆

Doc's advice

Patient went to his doctor and explained his problem was that he couldn't stop stealing things out of shops. Doctor explained that he was a kleptomaniac.

He gave him some pills and said, "Take three a day, and if they don't work, try and get me a colour telly!"

* * * * * *

I've got a pal who's a manio kleptic. He walks into shops backwards and leaves things!

* * * * * *

Record throw

At the last Olympic Games a big American contestant throws the hammer and beats the existing world record.

All the TV cameras and world's Press are clamouring around him.

He attributed his great strength to the fact that his father and brothers worked in the steel works and brought home large lumps of steel which he used for practice.

Next contestant was a Russian. He whacks the hammer 10 metres further than the American.

He attributed his strength to the fact that he worked in the salt mines and inhaling the salt fumes gave him great power.

Final contestant is a wee Glasgow fella. He lifts up the hammer and, with one hand in his pocket he throws the hammer 30 metres further than the Russian.

"An incredible throw, Willie," said the Press. "What do you attribute it to?"

"Well", said Willie, "Ma faither and a' ma brothers have been on the dole a' their lives, and ma faither gave me the best piece of advice anybody ever gave me.

"He said, 'If anybody ever hands you a hammer, son, throw it to hell as far away as possible'!"

"I DON'T THINK THIS IS A VERY GOOD PLACE, HERBERT NOBODY WILL BE ABLE TO SEE ANYTHING!"

"I'M NOT ALWAYS CRITICISING YOUR PRECIOUS CAR,
I'M ONLY ASKING ABOUT THE THUMPING NOISE".

It's a sign

☆ ☆ ☆

If you see chairs and tables on the pavement in Palma
or Paris they call it romantic. If you see that in
Glasgow, they call it eviction.

* * * ¢ * *

Draughty tale

A warrant was issued on behalf of a man who failed to
appear in court because of non payment of his rent.
A policeman was sent to hand over the warrant.
He arrived at the man's house and knocked on the door.
The man was in but, seeing the policeman, he kept
quiet and didn't answer the door.
So the policeman pushed the warrant through the
letter box.
However the man blew it back onto the doorstep.
This happened several times.
After half an hour the policeman tore up the warrant
saying to himself: "Dammit. If my house was as
draughty as this I wouldn't pay the rent either!"

"WE SEEM TO HAVE AN ABUNDANCE OF PORRIDGE, DARLING, DO YOU KNOW ANYONE WE COULD INVITE TO BREAKFAST?"

★ ★ ★

Oh no, Sydney

Sydney Devine has just released his latest LP — The Golden Voice of Scotland. It's got a 12 inch hole in it. It's the only label I've seen on a record where the wee dog's sitting with its paws clapped over its ears.

Hair today

I went to the barber the other day and told him my hair was falling out.
I asked him if he had something to keep it in.
So he gave me a cardboard box.

Pregnant pause

A young lady in our street said: "I would do ANYTHING for a fur coat." Now she's got one, she can't fasten it!

* * * * * *

* * * * * *

Tip for teacher

I remember the teacher came into the class and wrote on the board "I didn't have no fun on holiday last year."
"What should I do to correct that?" she said.
I said, "Take a fellow with you next year."

★ ★ ★

"IF IT DOESN'T WORK COME BACK AND I'LL MARRY YOU MYSELF!"

Pound foolish!

An Englishman and an Irishman were on the train.
The Englishman said: "Come on, just to pass the time
we'll have a quiz. I'll ask you a question, then you ask
me a question. If I can't answer your question, I'll give
you £5. You only have to give me £1 if you can't answer
my question. OK?"
"Right", said the Irishman, "I'll go first. What's got five
heads, fourteen legs, three tails and can't swim?"
The Englishman said, "I don't know. I just don't know;
here's you fiver. What is it?"
The Irishman said "There's your pound — I don't know
either."

☆   ☆   ☆

★   ★   ★

**"YOU SHOULD WEAR RUBBER GLOVES WHEN YOU
WASH THE DISHES!"**

"IT'S YOUR TURN TO CARRY ALBERT!"

☆　☆　☆

"IT'S TWENTY YEARS SINCE HE DID THAT WITH ME!"

Boxing clever!

I used to be a boxer. I was knocked out that many times, my wife had to count ten to get me up in the morning.

A passable drink!

Three Americans went into the chemist. The first American said, "I'd like something Scottish to drink". The chemist said, "I'm sorry sir, this isn't like a drug store back in America. We don't serve drinks in here." The American said, "How about that stuff on the shelf? Saint Andrew's liver salts — that sounds Scottish to me buddy."

The chemist thought, Why not, it's business, so he mixed up some salts.

The American downed them in one gulp.

"Bootiful!" he said. "I'll have another."

So the chemist mixed another glass.

The American downed it and called for another one for the road.

Then he asked the chemist, "Tell me, what does this stuff do for one?"

"Well," said the chemist, "it says on the label, with every glass taken, it makes you feel ten years younger."

"Ah", said the American, "That figures, I've just done a very childish thing."

Sailing ....

Yank sailor: Our boat's one of the fastest on the ocean waves. We have to stop to cool the propellers.
Wee Scottish cabin boy: That's nuthin'. Our boat's so fast we have to slow down to pick up radio messages!

Tall story ....

Dad: There's Dave. He's six feet in his socks.
Wee Jamie: Away, faither. Ye'll be tellin' me next that he's twa heids in his hat!

* * * * * *

Pregnant pause ....

Farmer: Ye're laddie Jake has gone too far this time. He went and got ma Jessie pregnant.
Neighbour: The careless twit. I'm always warning him tae be mair careful. Last week he broke the hay-foark!

The spirit's
willing but ....

An old man of 80 went to the chemist and asked for some of that stuff they used to put in boys' tea in the army.
The chemist said "Do you know what that stuff's for?"
'I'm fully aware of what it's for" replied the old man. "It was used to curb mens' passions."
"That's quite right," said the chemist.
"What does an old man like you want that stuff for?"
The old man said "I want to stuff it up my nose and get the ideas out of my head!"

"I LON'T FEEL CHEERED UP, GODFREY!"

Poor answer!

Fortune-teller: You will be in great poverty for the next 10 years of your life.
Hilda: Ah .... and then Lady Luck will smile on me?
Fortune-teller: No .... No, you'll just get used to the poverty.

....

Bad taste!

An Aberdonian stormed into a chemist's shop which was advertising half price medicine and shouted at the owner: "Ye canna dae this. I'm in perfect health!"

....

Fare's fair!

Train guard: What are you doing in here? This is a first class carriage.
Old Tramp: Aye, man, is it no' jist grand!

"HE CALLED ME A CHEAP CROOK — ME, WITH A SET-UP LIKE
THIS WITH POTTED PALMS AND EVERYTHING!"

Yawn, yawn!

Boring man: How long have I been speaking for? My watch
appears to have stopped.
Bored listener: It's easily checked. There's a calendar on the
wall!

Right Charlie!

*If Bonnie Prince Charlie was still alive today what would he
be famous for?*
Old age!

"I SUPPOSE HE COULD BE TARZAN —

HE'S BOUND TO BE GETTING ON A BIT!"

★ ★ ★

Quick sum!

What's the fastest way to say two hundred and fifty thousand four times?
A million!

"YOU'LL HAVE TO HELP ME WITH THE LOWER LINES.

MY EYESIGHT IS NOT WHAT IT USED TO BE!"